EXTREME LIFE CYCLES

CLOWN FISH

WRITTEN BY
E.C. ANDREWS

KidHaven PUBLISHING

Published in 2025 by
KidHaven Publishing, an Imprint of
Greenhaven Publishing, LLC
2544 Clinton St., Buffalo, NY 14224

Written by: E.C. Andrews
Edited by: Noah Leatherland
Designed by: Amelia Harris

Cataloging-in-Publication Data

Names: Andrews, E.C.
Title: Clown fish / E.C. Andrews.
Description: Buffalo, New York : KidHaven Publishing, 2025. | Series: Extreme life cycles | Includes glossary and index.
Identifiers: ISBN 9781534547018 (pbk.) | ISBN 9781534547025 (library bound) | ISBN 9781534547032 (ebook)
Subjects: LCSH: Anemonefishes--Juvenile literature. | Clown anemonefish--Life cycles--Juvenile literature.
Classification: LCC QL638.P77 A537 2025 | DDC 597'.72 --dc23

Manufactured in the United States of America

CPSIA compliance information: Batch #CSKH25
For further information contact Greenhaven Publishing LLC at 1-844-317-7404.

Please visit our website, www.greenhavenpublishing.com.
For a free color catalog of all our high-quality books, call toll free 1-844-317-7404 or fax 1-844-317-7405.

Find us on

IMAGE CREDITS

All images are courtesy of Shutterstock.com, unless otherwise specified. With thanks to Getty Images, Thinkstock Photo and iStockphoto. Cover – Josephine Julian. Recurring images – ReVelStockArt, Macrovector, Eightshot_Studio, ArtMari, Egor Shilov, Tartila, Miloje. 2 – Kurit afshen. 4–5 – Tartila. 6–7 – cbpix, Arunee Rodloy. 8–9 – JC Ten, Vojce. 10–11 – Gerald Robert Fischer, Bernard Lieu. 12–13 – Choksawatdikorn, Krzysztof Odziomek, Mayumi.K.Photography. 14–15 – FrentaN, Richard Whitcombe. 16–17 – Suphares Soilha, Daniel Lamborn. 18–19 – Daniel Lamborn, YUSRAN ABDUL RAHMAN. 20–21 – Joe Belanger, Thierry Eidenweil. 22–23 – Andrea Izzotti, Kurit afshen.

CONTENTS

Words that look like this can be found in the glossary on page 24.

WHAT IS A LIFE CYCLE?

All living things go through different stages in their lives. Their bodies change and grow. This is called a life cycle.

Most animals are small when they begin their lives. They grow up, get old, and one day, they die. During their lives, some animals might have offspring. This allows the life cycle to carry on.

WHAT IS A CLOWN FISH?

Clown fish are a small breed of fish. They live in the ocean. They are found in coral reefs. They need warm water and lots of places to hide.

Clown fish are very social. They even have a language of their own. They can communicate with each other by making clicking noises with their teeth.

EGGS

Clown fish start their lives as eggs. The mother clown fish lays her eggs on a hard surface. A mother clown fish can lay up to 1,500 eggs at once!

Clown fish live in anemones. Anemones have a poisonous sting, but clown fish are not hurt by it. The poisonous anemone protects the clown fish and their eggs from predators.

HATCHING

Clown fish are sneaky creatures right from the very moment they hatch. Clown fish eggs only hatch at night. They are in less danger of being eaten as most predators are asleep.

Baby clown fish are called fry. Clown fish fry are only 0.2 inch (0.5 cm) long when they hatch. Clown fish fry are translucent. This helps them hide from predators.

FRY

Clown fish fry spend the first 10 to 14 days of their lives floating around in the ocean. They eat tiny living things called plankton. This food helps them grow.

It takes about two weeks for clown fish to get their amazing white stripes. Having stripes means they are now young adults. They can now go and find an anemone to live in.

MALES AND FEMALES

Clown fish are not born as either male or female. But when clown fish grow up, something incredible happens! All the clown fish in a group become male, except for one. The largest one becomes a female.

Groups of fish are called shoals. Shoals of clown fish are led by one female. When the female leader dies, the largest male in the group changes into a female and becomes the new leader.

THE FEMALE CLOWN FISH

The female clown fish is in charge. She lays the eggs and makes sure the males are behaving themselves. She does this by being aggressive towards them. This reminds them that she is the boss!

To make sure she stays in charge, the female clown fish stops other male clown fish from becoming female. This means that she can keep her spot as the one female leader of the group.

THE MALE CLOWN FISH

While the female makes sure everyone is behaving themselves, the males have some rules of their own. They rank each other in order of size.

Once the clown fish have found an anemone to live in, a male clown fish helps the female prepare the nest. He does this by keeping their new home clean and tidy.

LAYING THE EGGS

The male clown fish helps the female find a hard surface to lay her eggs on. If there is not one in the nest, he will find one and bring it back to the anemone.

CLOWN FISH CAN USE SHELLS, ROCKS, AND CORAL TO LAY THEIR EGGS ON.

Once the female has laid the eggs, the male takes care of them. He makes sure the eggs stay clean, safe, and healthy. He also gets rid of any eggs that are broken.

THE CYCLE CARRIES ON

After the clown fish eggs have hatched, the males and female leave to start a new nest. The fry swim away and are left to look after themselves.

CLOWN FISH EGGS ALMOST READY TO HATCH

The clown fish fry grow up and become adults. They find an anemone to live in. They have babies of their own, just like their parents did. The whole cycle continues!

GLOSSARY

AGGRESSIVE having to do with acting in a forceful way

COMMUNICATE to pass information from one living thing to another

CORAL REEF an underwater habitat made up of the bodies of tiny animals

HATCH to come out of its egg

OFFSPRING the young of an animal or plant

POISONOUS able to make toxic matter that would be harmful if eaten or touched

PREDATOR an animal that hunts other animals for food

RANK to put in order of who is in charge

SOCIAL having to do with enjoying the company of others

TRANSLUCENT slightly see-through

INDEX